Happy Birthday, Garrett
2018

One-
Minute
Prayers™

Men

*God knows that you only
have one-minute at a time
these days!*

Text by Hope Lyda

*Love & Prayers Always,
Mother*

HARVEST HOUSE PUBLISHERS

EUGENE, OREGON

Cover by Garborg Design Works, Minneapolis, Minnesota

Cover photo © Getty Images

ONE-MINUTE PRAYERS™ FOR MEN
Copyright © 2004 by Harvest House Publishers
Eugene, Oregon 97402
www.harvesthousepublishers.com

ISBN 978-0-7369-1287-7

Printed in the United States of America

17 18 / BP-CF / 16 15 14

Contents

Because His Love Endures Forever

Give thanks to the LORD, for he is good. His love endures forever. Give thanks to the God of gods. His love endures forever. Give thanks to the Lord of lords: His love endures forever.

—PSALM 136:1-3

∽

Lord, thank You for the life You have given me. Upon rising in the morning, I worship the Lord of lords, the God of all gods, and the King of kings...and You call me by name. I think back to the day I met You and how You welcomed me with open arms. You received this prodigal son without hesitation.

For all these reasons and so many more, I give You thanks. I offer up my life to You and Your service. I can think of no greater way to live than to consider each day a holy, living sacrifice to You. May Your will be done through the course of my days.

Abilities

Use It

If a man's gift is prophesying, let him use it in proportion to his faith. If it is serving, let him serve; if it is teaching, let him teach; if it is encouraging, let him encourage; if it is contributing to the needs of other people, let him give generously; if it is leadership, let him govern diligently; if it is showing mercy, let him do it cheerfully.

—ROMANS 12:6-8

∽

God, thank You for the abilities You have bestowed on me. Along my journey I have faced times of ignoring, neglecting, and abusing my gifts. Forgive me for those times of ignorance. I do not want to disregard Your will in my life. I want to claim it and apply Your truth in all circumstances. I know this will involve using my abilities to serve You and other people.

Show me those gifts I have yet to discover. Show me the way to utilize the abilities I have acknowledged.

Going Beyond Ability

For I testify that they gave as much as they were able, and even beyond their ability. Entirely on their own, they urgently pleaded with us for the privilege of sharing in this service to the saints.

—2 CORINTHIANS 8:3-4

∽

Lord, don't let me hold onto my abilities as though they are mine to govern. When I can serve You by using the gifts You have given me, do not let me fight the opportunity because it involves too much time, energy, or commitment. Most of all, I pray to go beyond earthly expectations. I pray to move past the limitations set by human standards. Let me push forth in my work, my life, my faith, and serve You better.

It is a privilege to serve You and the body of Christ with my natural strengths. Let me keep this in mind as I face decisions and possibilities. May I always seek more ways to serve you, Lord.

Not for Sale

When Simon saw that the Spirit was given at the laying on of the apostles' hands, he offered them money and said, "Give me also this ability so that everyone on whom I lay my hands may receive the Holy Spirit."

—ACTS 8:18-19

❧

God, guide me toward Your great purpose in my life. Use me to serve the needs of other people in Your body and of Your creation. Let me not covet the success of other people because it causes me to want their gifts. When I see the achievements of other people, I begin to question my own status in the world. Lead me to a deeper, more meaningful understanding of Your plan, Lord.

When I am tempted to pursue at any cost a journey that is not meant to be mine, may I encounter the truth of Your Word, the wisdom of Your truth, and the wonder of my own life. I want to experience Your will, Lord, not the trappings of another person's path.

From the Same Source

There are different kinds of gifts, but the same Spirit. There are different kinds of service, but the same Lord. There are different kinds of working, but the same God works all of them in all men.

—1 CORINTHIANS 12:4-6

∼

Lord, as I make my way through each day, let me observe and appreciate the kaleidoscope of talent that is demonstrated by those I encounter. Humble my spirit so that I see past my abilities to those of people around me. May I see Your hand on their lives. May I see Your will being fulfilled in their actions.

You are the Source of all ability and talent, Lord. Please let me respect the gifts of other people. It is easy to focus only on my own journey. Lift my eyes beyond my private path to see the wonders You are performing all around me.

Provision

Where Greed Leads

A stingy man is eager to get rich and is unaware that poverty awaits him.

—PROVERBS 28:22

❧

In my quest to provide for myself and my family, Lord, may I not become greedy and selfish. It is very easy to lust for things of the world. I can lose sight of the spiritual priorities You set before me. My goal in life is not to accumulate "stuff" but to seek Your way. I do not want to seek material success that exceeds Your provision.

I have witnessed the downfall of colleagues and friends who desired more than they needed, more than You called them to possess. Everything I have is of You and from You. Never let my eyes or my hands search to claim more than what You provide at any given moment in time. I only want to be rich in spirit, Lord.

Behind Every Great Man

You may say to yourself, "My power and the strength of my hands have produced this wealth for me." But remember the LORD your God, for it is he who gives you the ability to produce wealth, and so confirms his covenant, which he swore to your forefathers, as it is today.

—DEUTERONOMY 8:17-18

∽

There is nothing in my life that does not come from You, Lord. Your blessings from heaven are responsible for my every possession, my every met need, my every reward. When success comes my way and brings provision for myself and other people, I turn to You with a heart of thanksgiving. You are my Source of strength and wealth.

You care for every one of Your children, Lord. I am so thankful to count myself among Your followers. May I use the provision of life and health and opportunity to serve You alone.

His Strength

If anyone serves, he should do it with the strength God provides, so that in all things God may be praised through Jesus Christ.

—1 PETER 4:11

∽

Lord, You see how my fears keep me from serving You fully. Let me put aside the insecurities that cripple me. Let me rely on the strength You provide so that I come to You every time I have a need. I want to fall at Your feet every time I face difficulty or conflict. I am shamed easily, Lord, because of my many inabilities. But I long to serve You with confidence and might.

Those who know me realize that my strength comes only from You, Lord. They have seen my weaknesses in the light of day and realize Your power is responsible for my every success. May this always be so. And may I always give You credit each time I show an ounce of strength, a bit of power, an inkling of understanding.

Fruit of a Good Life

*Our people must learn to devote themselves to
doing what is good, in order that they may provide
for daily necessities and not live unproductive lives.*

—TITUS 3:14

✌

The choice to do good is presented in so many
subtle ways, Lord. Sometimes it is not even a choice,
but an impulse—a nudge to follow in Your way. During
my day, keep me mindful of the opportunities I have to
do the right thing. May my life be an example to other
people. May my life be seen as productive in Your eyes.

I want to be prayerful throughout my day so I can
tap into Your leading at all times. This guidance is Your
provision. It directs my steps and shepherds me
through life.

Identity

Old Versus New Self

You were taught, with regard to your former way of life, to put off your old self, which is being corrupted by its deceitful desires; to be made new in the attitude of your minds; and to put on the new self, created to be like God in true righteousness and holiness.

—EPHESIANS 4:22-24

∽

God, I am so thankful You love Your creation. Instead of tossing us away with our collection of frailties, sins, and ungodly attitudes, You reach down and make us new beings. Our bruises and blemishes are not enough to turn Your eyes from us. You do not pass us up for better possibilities.

I am so humbled when I think of who I was before I met You. I still have days that reflect the old me, but now I can come to You with the burden of sin and seek Your forgiveness. I have experienced Your healing touch, and my heart has been transformed. May I resemble You more with each passing day.

Who Am I?

Who am I, O LORD God, and what is my family,
that you have brought me this far? And as if this
were not enough in your sight, O God, you have
spoken about the future of the house of your ser-
vant. You have looked on me as though I were the
most exalted of men, O LORD God.

—1 CHRONICLES 17:16-17

✍

My Christian life experience is a bit like climbing out of a canyon. The trek has been treacherous at times, and I have lost my footing, but I have kept my eyes focused on the summit of Your grace. Too many times I have been tempted to look down…back at the problems that tripped my feet, or at the crevices which lodged me in dark times. But as I climb higher, toward the Source of all light, I am comforted.

You lead me, Lord. You preserve me and my path. You have lifted me out of my sinful life. Why is it that You have brought me so far, Lord? May I reach for the stronghold of Your wisdom and continue along this way in gratitude.

Known

O LORD, you have searched me and you know me.
You know when I sit and when I rise; you perceive
my thoughts from afar.

—PSALM 139:1-2

❧

Lord, while I might keep to myself around other people, or limit what I share, I take great comfort in being vulnerable and open with You. You know every detail about me: how I am made, the ways in which I struggle, my deepest joys, and the future I will experience. There is such peace in being truly, completely known.

God, help me take this sense of security and turn it into confidence for my relationships with friends, family, and anyone I encounter. Keep me from putting up a facade to protect my heart or my pride. It is time to share the "real me" more openly with the body of Christ and those who do not know You. I seek Your strength as I work toward this goal.

Child of God

*This is how we know who the children of God are
and who the children of the devil are: Anyone who
does not do what is right is not a child of God; nor
is anyone who does not love his brother.*

—1 JOHN 3:10

❧

Lord, do I love enough? Do I pass along Your goodness to other people? I want to be known as a child of God. Where I am resistant to show love or express Your mercy, open up my heart. If I am quick to judge and slow to help another person, push me into action. I get so caught up trying to be who I am in the world that I forget how to be Your son.

I seek balance where these two identities should merge, Lord. Help me pare away characteristics and sins that do not represent You, my heavenly Father. Let me be Your hands and Your heart wherever I may go.

Asking for Directions

Finally, I Am Asking

Hear my cry, O God; listen to my prayer.

—PSALM 61:1

∽

My struggles lately have led me away from my Source of help: You. At first I thought I could figure out the answers on my own. But as I tried this, I lost my way and started to go deeper inside myself. I didn't even know how to ask people for assistance or advice, so I kept trying to get past my problems and failings. Each wrong turn and dead-end should have brought me back to You. Forgive me, Lord, for refusing to ask for help.

So here I am, finally calling out to You. Help me through this. Hear my cry, Lord. With humility I fall at Your feet and ask for guidance.

Within Your Reach

May your hand be ready to help me, for I have chosen your precepts.

—PSALM 119:173

෴

I choose Your ways, Lord. When I encounter difficulties, I rely on the guidance of Your precepts. Today I ask You to show me mercy, Lord. Reach down into my current circumstances and redirect my steps so that I stay true to Your will. It is easy to become sidetracked in this busy life. Lead me to ask for help as I need it.

I want to stay faithful to the path You have prepared for me. It is exciting to think about how You are using every day of my life to move me forward and to serve Your purpose.

Asking for Faith

Immediately the boy's father exclaimed, "I do believe; help me overcome my unbelief!"

—MARK 9:24

∽

God, I thank You for allowing me to have doubts even while I have faith. Your gift of free will also gives me room to experience a deep belief that becomes stronger through times of doubt. I ask You to overcome those moments, days, or even months of unbelief.

Thank You for sending people my way who have encouraged me to see You during hardship. The gift of faith is holy and precious. I pray that I will hold onto it tightly at all times, especially in the midst of doubt.

Pure Motivations

You do not have, because you do not ask God. When you ask, you do not receive, because you ask with wrong motives, that you may spend what you get on your pleasures.

—JAMES 4:2-3

∾

I have shaken my fists toward heaven, Lord. Forgive me for being demanding as I ask for things that do not match Your will. It is out of fear that I insist upon an answer...no...*the answer* that I want. I feel behind in my life...in the plans I made for myself. This selfish mode causes me to lose sight of Your wonderful purpose for my life.

Tear away from me this spirit of fear and arrogance, Lord. When I call to You, let my spirit of repentance be sincere. Let my requests be in line with Your plan. And when my fears override my understanding of how You work, quiet my heart so I can hear Your words of leading.

Cooperation

Neighborly Behavior

Therefore each of you must put off falsehood and speak truthfully to his neighbor, for we are all members of one body.

—EPHESIANS 4:25-26

∽

God, rid my language of little white lies—of half-truths that make the moment easier. Let my exchanges with strangers and coworkers be as honest as those I have at home and church. I pray for the wise man's ability to think before speaking. I have been bound by less-than-truthful comments or by gossip, and I know these never end well.

May I never place my pride above truth. May I treat every person with the respect I have for those closest to me. Better yet, I will speak to other people in truth as I do to You.

Called to Peace

Let the peace of Christ rule in your hearts, since as
members of one body you were called to peace.

—COLOSSIANS 3:15

༶

While I try to lead a meaningful and purposeful life, Lord, I know that much of my busyness is caused by insignificant pursuits. I get uptight about little matters and let them fill my heart with anxiety. Release me from these trivial ties to earthly concerns. Pull my thoughts inward and my prayers upward so that I can cooperate with Your Spirit during these times.

I have the eternal Source of peace within me because of Your gift of salvation. May I never take You for granted. Let my success be measured by how well I reflect Your peace to other people in the body of Christ and beyond it.

Seeing Your Work in Others

*In all my prayers for all of you, I always pray with
joy because of your partnership in the gospel from
the first day until now, being confident of this, that
he who began a good work in you will carry it on to
completion until the day of Christ Jesus.*

—PHILIPPIANS 1:4-6

✑

God, my insecurities can rise to the surface when I
face competition in any arena. I put in a lot of time and
am very committed to my job, but this effort should
never distort my view of other people and their worth.

Let me see in all people the good work You have
begun in their hearts. Let that be how I relate to them
at all times...as a fellow child of God, not as a com-
petitor or opponent. Serving You and the church
requires my commitment to kindness and graciousness.
Lead me to encourage other people and look for the
good in them at all times.

Hurdling Sin

You are still worldly. For since there is jealousy and quarreling among you, are you not worldly? Are you not acting like mere men?

—1 CORINTHIANS 3:3-4

∽

Sin sure can get in the way of a cooperative spirit, Lord. Sometimes, instead of praying about my sins and repenting, I hurdle them and try to keep going forward. Show me how futile this is, Lord. Jealousy and a quick temper hinder my abilities and also the ways in which You can work through my life. I become the hurdle to Your will being accomplished.

As a man, I will sin. As a child of God, I will seek and find forgiveness so I can stay true to the path of eternity that is placed before me.

Silence

A Patient Heart

The LORD is good to those whose hope is in him, to the one who seeks him; it is good to wait quietly for the salvation of the LORD.

—LAMENTATIONS 3:25-26

❧

With hope in my heart, I can wait upon Your mercy, Lord. My mouth, so used to forming a string of words, of wants, of grievances, can be closed and still. My voice, so used to crying out, requesting, questioning, can be silenced.

Surrounded by hope, there is no need for the noise of the human mind and heart. Prayers pour forth from my soul. God, thank You for the sanctuary created by the void of words. Encourage me to return to this place more often. When the busy days shout their commands, I will return to Your feet and be thankful for the quiet.

Goodness Silences Ignorance

For it is God's will that by doing good you should silence the ignorant talk of foolish men.

—1 PETER 2:15

∽

God, the words spoken in haste by another person seem to have such an impact on me. When a person throws around harsh words in a careless manner, help me see that it is usually ignorance or lack of attention and not evil behind the recklessness.

God, my security is in You. I do not need the validation of other people. Let me turn my concern into prayers for that person's well-being. May I act out a living prayer by responding to strong words with gentle kindness.

Quiet Wisdom

The quiet words of the wise are more to be heeded
than the shouts of a ruler of fools.

—ECCLESIASTES 9:17

∽

Lord, help me stay true to what is right when I am tempted to step out of wisdom and enter the arena of fools. In a meeting the other day I was barely able to voice my opinion while other people freely spoke up, took over, and filled the time for their purposes. Each time I was cut off, my frustration was fueled.

But then You tugged at my heart. I did say what I wanted to express and that was enough. There was no need to compete with their numerous comments and cranked-up volume. You allowed me to remain calm and in control of myself. Thank You for reminding me that You hear every word I speak.

The Hush of Humility

For it is by grace you have been saved, through faith—and this not from yourselves, it is the gift of God—not by works, so that no one can boast.

—EPHESIANS 2:8-9

∽

God, everything I have is from You. The faith I hold onto tightly is a gift of Your grace. If people see the peace and wholeness of my life, may I never claim responsibility for such things. I will share about Your mercy. I will share how Your love transformed me at a time when I could do nothing to help myself.

My dependence on You should shine far brighter than my self-sufficiency. Let everything I do, say, accomplish, or receive praise for be a reflection of Your gift.

Communication

If You Can't Say Anything Nice...

Come, my children, listen to me; I will teach you the fear of the LORD. Whoever of you loves life and desires to see many good days, keep your tongue from evil and your lips from speaking lies.

—PSALM 34:11-13

༂

"Bite your tongue." That is what my mother used to tell me to do when a lie or mean comment was about to slip out of my young mouth. God, You offer me the same advice, and I would be wise to heed it. I believe also that when I am struggling to hold back an unnecessary dig or sarcastic comment, I should look for something good to say at the moment—something righteous and sincere.

Lord, direct my tongue to share the good news. And when that does not surface easily in the heat of the moment, let me fall silent and spend my energy listening for Your direction and awaiting Your peace.

Prayers Translated

We do not know what we ought to pray for, but the Spirit himself intercedes for us with groans that words cannot express.

—ROMANS 8:26

&

Lord, I fumble along in conversations that have little true significance; therefore, I am so thankful the Spirit intercedes for me when I am at a loss for words. My brokenness cannot be translated into syllables. I can only moan in the midst of darkness. And You are able to decipher every bit of meaning.

The other day, I could not cry or speak. The only sound was that of my heart pounding strongly in my chest. And I knew You understood every beat.

Tell It to Me Straight

Then Jesus' disciples said, "Now you are speaking clearly and without figures of speech. Now we can see that you know all things and that you do not even need to have anyone ask you questions. This makes us believe that you came from God."

—JOHN 16:29-30

∽

Like the disciples who stood by and listened to Your parables and stories and could not fully discern Your truth, I need things spelled out sometimes. I ask You for clear direction in my life right now, Lord. I turn to Your Word for wisdom and am so thankful for its power. I pray that I will be sensitive enough to hear Your messages that are just for me.

In my life, I witness how You guide my steps and lead my heart. My history reveals how personally Your truth impacts my life. The message of Your love becomes very clear…and I know You are God.

Words for Good

Reckless words pierce like a sword, but the tongue of the wise brings healing.

—PROVERBS 12:18

❧

Lord, as I go about my day, let me be watching for the people who need a healing word. Help me to listen to the needs being expressed around me. At work, while business is the topic, encourage my spirit to also listen to what individuals are saying beneath that conversation. Is their life difficult right now? Are they excited about a recent joyful event?

Every conversation I have with another person is important. The exchange of friendly banter or deep discussions about faith and life...they all matter because these dialogues connect me with other beings created in Your image. Remind me, Lord, to be an encourager.

Learning to Be

How to Live

Make it your ambition to lead a quiet life, to mind
your own business and to work with your hands,
just as we told you, so that your daily life may win
the respect of outsiders and so that you will not be
dependent on anybody.

—1 THESSALONIANS 4:11-12

ॐ

God, You created life to be a process of growing and
becoming. Learning how to live becomes a lifelong
journey. Just when I think I have arrived at the place
where You will surely have me stay, change happens
and I am prodded to go further.

As You call me to keep moving and growing, I abide
by the guidelines You offer in Your Word. I lead a quiet
life focused on You. I mind my own business and strive
to earn the respect of other people by working hard.
And each day I renew my commitment to walk in Your
will.

Resting in the Lord

*On this day, atonement will be made for you, and
you will be cleansed from all your sins in the LORD's
presence. It will be a Sabbath day of total rest, and
you will spend the day in fasting.*

—LEVITICUS 16:30-31 (NLT)

∽

Lord, lead my spirit in the exercise of rest today. I
feel a bit anxious, and my mind keeps visiting all of the
tasks I have to do. But I long to rediscover the practice
of the Sabbath. The world teaches me that I will fall
behind or lose my place if I take time to just "be." But
You call me to take time out for renewal.

May I use my determination to schedule my days to
serve the purpose of the Sabbath. Lead me to be diligent
in this discipline. I pray that I will learn to rest in You.

Every Day
a New Beginning

In the morning, O Lord, you hear my voice; in the morning I lay my requests before you and wait in expectation.

—PSALM 5:3

%

I love the morning, Lord. Thank You for allowing me to experience a beginning every day of my life. Before my mind turns to the many scheduled items for the day, I feel the peace of Your presence. When I wake up early and the light of day is just starting to warm the earth around me, there is a sense of awe that overcomes my spirit.

Grant me this feeling of serenity when I am overwhelmed. When activity replaces a spirit of meditation and prayer, restore my gratitude from the day's beginning.

Being Myself

The LORD God formed the man from the dust of the ground and breathed into his nostrils the breath of life, and the man became a living being.

—GENESIS 2:7

∽

Your hand is responsible for forming the physical shape of mankind. Lord, Your breath entered a form and turned it into a living being. Help me to embrace this breath of life...this living spirit that resides within me. You created wonderful, active beings as Your children.

You could have insisted that we look the same, act the same, and follow one path...but You didn't. Instead, You formed each of us as an individual. You breathed life into our lungs and souls, and we became our unique selves. Lord, thank You for letting me be myself.

Trust

Share the Load

*Trust in him at all times, O people; pour out your
hearts to him, for God is our refuge.*

—PSALM 62:8

∽

I give You the concerns of my heart today, Lord. You
know the burdens I am carrying right now. They weigh
on my mind and turn my waking moments into
chances to worry. I believe You are my Refuge. I do. I
just have not allowed You to play that role when it
comes to this particular worry. Why do I hold back so
much?

I want to trust You with everything in my life. Help
me lighten my grip on matters of insignificance. And in
matters of great importance and spiritual weight, let me
be free to turn them over to You, my Provider, my Lord,
my Rock.

God-Reliance

*Indeed, in our hearts we felt the sentence of death.
But this happened that we might not rely on our-
selves but on God, who raises the dead.*

—2 CORINTHIANS 1:9

∽

Lord, when I ponder my humanity, my mortality, it is easy to become stressed about my limitations. People around me seek ways to live forever, yet they are missing the truth of Your gift. I am so thankful I have received Your Son and eternity. Now, please guide me to trust this gift. Give my heart assurance that today is about my life here on earth, and Your plan for my tomorrow is also in the works.

God, I rely on Your provision to make it through daily life. Remind my spirit to have this same reliance on Your provision of eternal life.

Nothing Can
Stop Me Now

He will have no fear of bad news; his heart is stead-fast, trusting in the LORD.

—PSALM 112:7

∽

Lord, lately I have been waiting for the proverbial other shoe to drop. I faced some difficulties, and now I am afraid to trust You with what could happen next. My body feels tight with anticipation of further hardship rather than blessing.

The world tells me that struggle is a sign of weakness or is the fruit of failure. But because I know You and Your ways, I understand how trials are blessings. My dependence on You becomes a life of freedom. I am moving forward today. I trust Your will, Lord.

Truth Leads to Trust

Love does not delight in evil but rejoices with the truth. It always protects, always trusts, always hopes, always perseveres.

—1 CORINTHIANS 13:6-7

∽

God, in my relationships with other people, help me present You truthfully. I want my family to be able to trust me completely. I pray I will always be able, with Your strength, to protect them, give them hope, and lead them through the hard times. When they turn to me for reassurance, may I turn their hearts to Your hope.

I do not know any way through this life except to follow You each day. You guide my steps. Sometimes they are steps meant for me alone. At other times they are steps intended to set the way for other people. Lord, find my heart trusting and my spirit willing.

Real Manhood

Learning from Others

Uzziah was sixteen years old when he became king, and he reigned in Jerusalem fifty-two years. His mother's name was Jecoliah; she was from Jerusalem. He did what was right in the eyes of the LORD, just as his father Amaziah had done. He sought God during the days of Zechariah, who instructed him in the fear of God. As long as he sought the LORD, God gave him success.

—2 CHRONICLES 26:3-5

∽

I pray to understand the importance of being a man...a man of God. I turn to You with my needs, my praises, my thanksgiving. Yet I often turn to ungodly examples of manhood. There are so many images and idols that sway my good intentions from Your will to false truths.

Direct me toward mentorship with a godly man. Give me discernment as I weigh the choices of my life. I pray for Your leading so I can read words written by men of God, listen to the lessons of these men, and emulate those who live a righteous, holy life. I long to be the man You created me to be.

Just Look at My Father

This is the written account of Adam's line. When God created man, he made him in the likeness of God.

—GENESIS 5:1

༄

Lord, what do You see in me that reflects You? As I go about my day, are there moments when You shine through? I pray this is so. Have my many efforts to succeed as a man steered me away from my Father's ways? Lord, lead me back on track. Present me with the challenge to become more like You in all things.

Right now I need patience and understanding. I need reassurance of my Father's love. You have blessed me in so many ways. Let me count these blessings and pray over my life so that the security of Your love fills my heart. Thank You for caring about me, for creating me and providing Your Son as a model of manhood and godliness.

I Am a Son

Because you are sons, God sent the Spirit of his Son into our hearts, the Spirit who calls out, "Abba, Father." So you are no longer a slave, but a son; and since you are a son, God has made you also an heir.

—GALATIANS 4:6-7

❧

How I want to resemble my heavenly Father! Lord, as You formed man and woman, what did You wish for Your children? I want to live my life in a way that is pleasing to You. I want to walk and talk with the grace and wisdom of Abba. Open my eyes to how I can be more like You during times of rest, in moments of interaction, and at points of decision.

My earthly father has taught me many things. As I continue to grow in my adult life, I look to You to teach me the ways of heaven and holiness.

Caring for My Life

Show me, O LORD, my life's end and the number of my days; let me know how fleeting is my life. You have made my days a mere handbreadth; the span of my years is as nothing before you. Each man's life is but a breath.

—PSALM 39:4-5

∽

God, it is so amazing how I can rest in the truth that my life is just a breath in Your eternal plan. But I do find peace in this understanding. It means my days are part of a whole picture. I am insignificant compared to Your greatness, but I am significant because I am Yours. My days count in the unfolding of mankind. My family history and my family's future are connected to Your master plan.

With each breath I take into my lungs, fill me with the desire to care for my life. I want to consider it precious and meaningful. Show me how to please You, Lord, with all that I have and with all that I am.

Vocation

Future Plans

For we are God's workmanship, created in Christ Jesus to do good works, which God prepared in advance for us to do.

—EPHESIANS 2:10

∾

My finger is double-jointed. My face shows the wear of past years. My voice is used to praise You. You know and see all of this because I am the creation of Your hands. My heart beats in a rhythm designed by You. Use me, Lord. Lead me toward the good works You wish to entrust to this child.

As You formed me, You blessed me with plans for a future. I don't want to miss out on any of the exciting changes, opportunities, and blessings You have in store for me. Where I am resistant to follow, Lord, give me a change of mind and heart. Draw my spirit closer to the Spirit so I walk in communion with Christ.

Show Me the Purpose

So neither he who plants nor he who waters is anything, but only God, who makes things grow. The man who plants and the man who waters have one purpose, and each will be rewarded according to his own labor. For we are God's fellow workers; you are God's field, God's building.

—1 CORINTHIANS 3:7-9

⌒

Show me the purpose, Lord. When I head to work or return home, fill me with Your wisdom. When I am centered in Your will, I feel it, Lord. It doesn't mean that all is going well. In fact, I have found my trust strengthened during the trials. Don't let me give up on the calling You have prepared for me.

As I work with other people, let me reflect on their purpose and contribution. Let me praise them for their good works and thank You for their efforts. We are all a part of the body You have formed. Led by Christ, we are called to find the way of righteousness and integrity. I make this my goal and my pledge to You, Lord.

Prize in Sight

*Brothers, I do not consider myself yet to have taken
hold of it. But one thing I do: Forgetting what is
behind and straining toward what is ahead, I press
on toward the goal to win the prize for which God
has called me heavenward in Christ Jesus.*

—**PHILIPPIANS 3:13-14**

∽

I have returned to my past recently for a visit. For
days I have been carrying around some regrets that I
thought I had given over to You long ago. I don't want
to spend time with these ghosts, Lord. I want to leave the
past behind me and press on toward the goal of purpose.

I know that I cannot fully embrace the next step in
my life until I release my past worries to Your care. I do
not look at my faith as a system of rewards, but I do see
the prize of eternity ahead. It glimmers and reflects Your
radiant grace. It inspires me to be steady, hardworking,
and aware of Your calling every day.

The Job of Holiness

*As obedient children, do not conform to the evil
desires you had when you lived in ignorance. But
just as he who called you is holy, so be holy in all you
do; for it is written: "Be holy, because I am holy."*

—1 PETER 1:14-16

∽

This holiness thing is work. I am forgiven because
of Your grace. I did nothing to earn that gift. But the
quest for holiness is not easy. I am paring away the
places of my life that counter this purpose. I have had
to step away from former associates who brought me
down. You revealed a sin in my life that was blocking
my growth. I am understanding that this pursuit will
indeed involve effort.

Keep me pure and energized, Lord. I want to be up
for the task and ready for the challenges You place
before me.

Freedom

I Am in a Jam

Listen to my cry, for I am in desperate need; rescue me from those who pursue me, for they are too strong for me. Set me free from my prison, that I may praise your name.

—PSALM 142:6-7

✺

My enemies might not resemble those faced by biblical warriors, but I do have enemies. There are attackers of my time, my well-being, my happiness. The quest for money, jealousy, blind ambition, reckless talk…these enemies stalk my spirit and wear it down. I feel the oppression in my gut. Some of these enemies were as familiar as friends, so it was hard to turn from them. I realize I have not moved far enough away and am vulnerable.

Help me use Your strength to fight these lurking foes, Lord. Arm me with Your Word, Your truth, and Your peace. I will praise Your name.

The Harm of Want

Keep your lives free from the love of money and be content with what you have, because God has said, "Never will I leave you; never will I forsake you."

—HEBREWS 13:5

၅

If someone asked me point-blank, "Would you trade the security of God's presence for the security of great wealth?" I would say no. Yet, Lord, I find that my daily decisions reflect the opposite of that adamant no. I am lacking contentment in my life right now. I am easily displeased when plans for my money and possessions are ruined.

God, direct my decisions and my heart so that my life is in line with Your will. I will only find freedom when I release the burden of material accumulation into Your hands. Let me discover the joy found in what You want for my life.

Not for Sale

*The Spirit and the bride say, "Come!" And let him
who hears say, "Come!" Whoever is thirsty, let him
come; and whoever wishes, let him take the free gift
of the water of life.*

—REVELATION 22:17

❧

In this culture of comparison shopping and making
deals, Your gift of eternal life is easy to question. I'm
sorry, Lord, but it is difficult to truly "sell" a real deal
anymore without provoking skepticism. We are trained
to doubt something that is too good to be true. And
surely the gift of life is that. What we forget is that You
are not too good to be true; You are the Spirit of goodness, the Creator of kindness and mercy.

God, help me show other people how genuine Your
gift is. If they do not see evidence of Your salvation in
my life, they will forever question the authenticity of my
claims. I want to become the one who invites other
people to drink of Your mercy absolutely free of charge.

The Prison of Judgment

Do not judge, and you will not be judged. Do not condemn, and you will not be condemned. Forgive, and you will be forgiven. Give, and it will be given to you. A good measure, pressed down, shaken together and running over, will be poured into your lap. For with the measure you use, it will be measured to you.

—LUKE 6:37-38

&

Lord, when did You put me in charge of judging all my brothers in Christ? Never. That is what I thought. So why do I pretend to sit on a higher moral ground than other people? God, this is a lonely place to be anyway. I don't want to be eager to tear down another child of God. I want to be a builder of Your kingdom.

Free me from the prison of my judgment so that I can receive and share Your grace. I want to give a good measure of grace so I can in turn receive a good measure back from Your heart.

Fatherhood

A God for
All Generations

May the LORD our God be with us as he was with our fathers; may he never leave us nor forsake us. May he turn our hearts to him, to walk in all his ways and to keep the commands, decrees and regulations he gave our fathers.

—1 KINGS 8:57-58

∽

You are the God of my father and of those men in my life whom I count as mentors. I thank You for the gift of salvation that ties me to prior generations. As I reflect on my lineage, I know it is not the blood of my family line that makes me who I am, but the blood of Christ.

God, give me a heart for You that beats so strong and so pure that it resounds in my children. Let my legacy be one of faith. Order my priorities so my children feel precious and loved, so I can introduce them to what it feels like to be Your child.

A Daily Choice

Fix these words of mine in your hearts and minds; tie them as symbols on your hands and bind them on your foreheads. Teach them to your children, talking about them when you sit at home and when you walk along the road, when you lie down and when you get up.

—DEUTERONOMY 11:18-19

೨∕ಾ

Being a good father is a daily choice, Lord—or rather, a string of choices. I practice the art of patience, the discipline of disciplining, and the forced skill of multitasking all before breakfast. I rely on the wisdom of Your Word to show me how to interact with my children in a godly way. I share verses with them so they, too, can understand my Source of knowledge and peace.

Being a father and being a child of God require the same degree of attention and priority. My diligence in growing my faith directly affects my efforts to grow my children. Lord, thank You for the model of Your fatherly love.

Staying Pure

I will walk in my house with blameless heart. I will set before my eyes no vile thing.

—PSALM 101:2-3

༼

Keep me pure, Lord. There are many distractions in the world today. The vices of many people are presented as not only okay but healthy. There is such a discrepancy between society's standards and Your own. Help me guard my heart and life from sinful desires so I can enter my home and return to my family with a clean, righteous spirit.

Building a family requires great trust. Lord, may my family always be able to depend on me to be a man of integrity, vulnerability, and honesty. As You hear my requests for forgiveness, Lord, protect me so I can remain blameless and worthy of my loving family.

Team Teaching

*All your sons will be taught by the LORD, and great
will be your children's peace.*

—ISAIAH 54:13

∽

God, last week I faced a moment when I just didn't
feel adequate to be guiding my children through life.
There are so many things I do not understand about the
world and about how You work in the world. The question that filled me with worry was, "What if they need
help or answers that I am not able to give them?"

Then You reminded me that You, too, have a vested
interest in the lives of my children. My children are Your
children. Your concern for their knowledge and fulfillment surpasses even my own. My job is not to be their
only teacher, but to direct them in all ways to You, the
Creator and Teacher of all good things.

Integrity

Live and Learn

He who ignores discipline despises himself, but whoever heeds correction gains understanding. The fear of the LORD teaches a man wisdom, and humility comes before honor.

—PROVERBS 15:32-33

❧

Lord, open my heart up to correction. When I receive fair guidance from another person, I become defensive or embarrassed. I hold back from saying anything about my feelings, but later I dwell on that sense of failure rather than on the tools I have been given to do a better job. Let me trust that Your hand is on me and the circumstances so I will be receptive to the lessons You are teaching me.

God, I want to be a humble man with integrity in all areas of my life. Let me be as eager to receive instruction as I am to receive praise. The next time I face this situation, I will lean on You for strength.

Starving the Ego

It is not good to eat too much honey, nor is it honorable to seek one's own honor. Like a city whose walls are broken down is a man who lacks self-control.

—PROVERBS 25:27-28

∽

Oh, Lord. As I experience success in different ways, I pray I will always give You the glory. Keep my head level. Help me not to become bloated with pride and false importance. It is so easy to feed on the sweetness of compliments rather than on the hard kernels of Your truth.

God, build up my self-control so I am protected from the desire to stuff my ego with empty words. I pray that You see me as a person of substance and integrity. Let my honor come from my association with the King of kings.

Moving Toward Good Things

For the LORD God is a sun and shield; the LORD bestows favor and honor; no good thing does he withhold from those whose walk is blameless.

—PSALM 84:11

෨

God, Giver of all that is good, You are the Source of the grace that flows through my veins and keeps me alive. Your strength moves me toward good things. I work to hold my head up high, not with pride, but with honor that comes from the faith life.

Keep me in line with Your will. Push, tug, and lead me toward the future You have for me. When I am not making progress toward Your blessings, it is not because You are withholding them. It is because I have not yet moved toward Your will. Do not let me stray from the goodness that awaits, Lord.

Success

Money Versus Value

*What good is it for a man to gain the whole world,
and yet lose or forfeit his very self?*

—LUKE 9:25

∾

Lord, I caught myself planning how my money could multiply over the years, and not once did I think about Your provision and plan. Please help me to find a balance as I strive for success. Present me with Your definition of successful living so I do not equate my earnings and my future portfolio with true value.

I have seen how money destroys people. God, do not let me rest in monetary securities. You are my Provider and the Creator of my life strategy. May I become excited as I imagine how my current blessings will multiply as I learn to trust You.

Take the High Road

"For my thoughts are not your thoughts, neither are your ways my ways," declares the LORD. *"As the heavens are higher than the earth, so are my ways higher than your ways and my thoughts than your thoughts."*

—ISAIAH 55:8-9

ের্

My earthly perspective is in the trenches right now. Lord, pull me out of this place and lift my thoughts to a higher plane so I begin to see life as You do. What started as a rut became a chasm that limited my ability to succeed or move forward in Your will. Please forgive me for thinking You would be limited by the walls of that trench. I forgot that You are God.

When You bring me home to heaven, I will already know the feeling of rising above my human circumstances, because today You lifted me up and showed me, once again, that You are my God.

Practice Makes Perfect

So if you have not been trustworthy in handling worldly wealth, who will trust you with true riches? And if you have not been trustworthy with someone else's property, who will give you property of your own?

—LUKE 16:11-12

&

In my early years of adulthood, I was not a very good steward, Lord. You had given me numerous blessings, opportunities, and elements of value which I abused or squandered. Then I had years of want and regret. Now I see Your hand guiding me once again toward success and ownership. You do not call me to great wealth, but now I understand how to be a steward of each and every blessing.

God, let me seek wise counsel in matters of money and property so I can serve You and Your body with such blessings. And may I always seek Your counsel as I make decisions about the biggest blessing of all: the gift of life.

Building a Life

Now, my son, the LORD be with you, and may you have success and build the house of the LORD your God, as he said you would. May the LORD give you discretion and understanding when he puts you in command over Israel, so that you may keep the law of the LORD your God.

—1 CHRONICLES 22:11-12

✎

I have heard many speakers on the topics of success and life management. Those that have the most influence on me are those who are unknowingly borrowing material from the true source: You and Your Word. Even non-Christians understand the importance of starting with a solid foundation to build a solid life.

God, make my life a house of the Lord. Guide me to use strong, worthy materials as I heed Your instruction for each step. The process involves determination, prayer, and sweat. But because my Cornerstone is Christ, this is a life worth building.

True Strength

Giving In and Getting Strong

Love the LORD *your God with all your heart and
with all your soul and with all your strength.*

—DEUTERONOMY 6:5

࿇

As a guy, I once equated love with weakness. I guess
that came from the idea of going "weak in the knees" or
"falling head over heels." But, God, it was finding and
accepting Your love that changed my view of human
love.

Giving up control and giving in to Your love became
the start of true strength in my life. Opening up my
heart and soul to Your love allowed me to lean upon
Your understanding and will. Standing alone without
the structure of faith is weakness. Thank You for a new
definition and understanding of strength.

Weakness Works

When I came to you, brothers, I did not come with eloquence or superior wisdom as I proclaimed to you the testimony about God. For I resolved to know nothing while I was with you except Jesus Christ and him crucified. I came to you in weakness and fear, and with much trembling. My message and my preaching were not with wise and persuasive words, but with a demonstration of the Spirit's power, so that your faith might not rest on men's wisdom, but on God's power.

—1 CORINTHIANS 2:1-5

℘

People fear public speaking, and I don't blame them, Lord. There seems to be nothing worse than fumbling through words while the eyes of many people focus on me. I need to think about my status as a humble messenger in life. You can speak through my words and my actions if I give myself over to You.

I will accept this role of messenger and present what I need to say in my very human, imperfect way, because my weakness magnifies Your greatness. My humanity allows Your divinity to shine forth.

He Is Strong

*But he said to me, "My grace is sufficient for you,
for my power is made perfect in weakness." Therefore I will boast all the more gladly about my weaknesses, so that Christ's power may rest on me. That
is why, for Christ's sake, I delight in weaknesses, in
insults, in hardships, in persecutions, in difficulties.
For when I am weak, then I am strong.*

—2 CORINTHIANS 12:9-10

∽

I am weak, but You are strong. Yes, Jesus loves me, and I love Him. While having a list of weaknesses a mile long is not always a comforting thought, I finally understand why I am human and You are God. I don't like to shine a light on my failings, but I have learned to release them to You so You can use them to reveal Your might.

Thank You for giving me the freedom to have my identity in You. This allows me to showcase my weaknesses, give You credit for my moments of strength, and direct attention to Your grace. It is not about me. It is about You working through me. And as I rid myself of ego, I can be filled by the power of Your Spirit.

I've Got the Power

*And we pray this in order that you may live a life
worthy of the Lord and may please him in every
way: bearing fruit in every good work, growing in
the knowledge of God, being strengthened with all
power according to his glorious might so that you
may have great endurance and patience, and joy-
fully giving thanks to the Father, who has qualified
you to share in the inheritance of the saints in the
kingdom of light.*

—COLOSSIANS 1:10-12

✍

God, I praise You for the life You have given me.
When it bears fruit, it is because Your power has made
it capable of goodness. If a pleasing harvest is brought
forth from my life, I have energy and health in my body
and spirit. I feel the power of You moving through me
and my circumstances in order to bring Your plan to
fruition.

My inheritance is a bountiful landscape. And in
times of drought, I don't need to ask whether to continue working the fields. You call me to be strong...but
not strong and alone, for I have Your power in my life
to carry me through all seasons.

Management

All in the Family

He must manage his own family well and see that his children obey him with proper respect. (If anyone does not know how to manage his own family, how can he take care of God's church?)

—1 TIMOTHY 3:4-5

&

God, the family unit is my measure of true success. How I am doing within and for my family directly relates to how successful I am in other areas. If I power my way through the business world, yet do not have the respect of my children, I am not a man of stature but am a failure. God, forgive me if I am ever tempted to choose worldly success over the well-being of my family.

I pray for my friends who struggle with their home life. It gives them an even sharper, more desperate edge in the workplace. But the efforts of their hands and minds become a house of cards instead of a substantial offering of stone. Lord, encourage me and my friends to put first things first and manage our homes in a way that is pleasing to You.

If They Could
See Me Now

*For though I am absent from you in body, I am
present with you in spirit and delight to see how
orderly you are and how firm your faith in Christ is.*

—COLOSSIANS 2:5

≈

God, if my mentors and encouragers of the past
could see my life now, would they be pleased? Those
people who helped me grow in my faith early on...
would they be delighted by how I manage everything
from home to work to relationships? I pray to be able to
observe my life from a distance once in a while so I can
notice the areas where I need You all the more.

I pray my life is firmly in order. As I pray for this
structure, I also pray that I am willing to change course
at a moment's notice if it is Your will. Those who touched
my life in the past would not want me to ever put my
plans before Your own. I long to please You, Lord.

Pick Me

The Lord answered, "Who then is the faithful and wise manager, whom the master puts in charge of his servants to give them their food allowance at the proper time? It will be good for that servant whom the master finds doing so when he returns."

—LUKE 12:42-43

～

Okay, God. I have been known to bite off more than I can chew. One success can go to my head so fast that I forget to thank You for the milestone and ask how to best use it. I pray You understand my eagerness to accomplish things. I pray You see through my childish impatience and look at my potential ability to serve You well.

I set my sights on work that pleases You. I do not earn Your grace, Lord, but I want to be worthy of the moment when You choose me to handle a responsibility. If You entrust me with an opportunity to do good, may You not be disappointed.

Part of a Whole

Now the body is not made up of one part but of many. If the foot should say, "Because I am not a hand, I do not belong to the body," it would not for that reason cease to be part of the body. And if the ear should say, "Because I am not an eye, I do not belong to the body," it would not for that reason cease to be part of the body....But in fact God has arranged the parts in the body, every one of them, just as he wanted them to be.

—1 CORINTHIANS 12:14-18

∽

God, the best managers are those who acknowledge the worth and contribution of every person they supervise. The best coaches are those who observe and utilize the strengths of every team member. Give me this mindset when I am put in charge of shepherding any group. Whether I am serving on a committee at church or participating in a workplace discussion, let me clearly see the value of each person there.

You see the beauty and originality of all of us, Lord. May I have Your eyes when looking into the eyes of another person. And then let me notice how that person resembles You.

Leading

The Way Everlasting

Search me, O God, and know my heart; test me and know my anxious thoughts. See if there is any offensive way in me, and lead me in the way everlasting.

—PSALM 139:23-24

❧

Do I offend You in any way, Lord? When I read the Old Testament, it seems Your followers were eager to have their hearts known and their evil ways pointed out. Call me to this place of willingness, God. I am reluctant to know my faults, so it is difficult to ask You to make them apparent. Yet, I want to be a healthy, informed servant so I can be led.

So lead me, Lord, to the way everlasting. Along the journey, reveal to me the secrets of my heart that even I do not know. Unveil the sins that keep me from better days.

Follow the Leader

Teach me to do your will, for you are my God; may your good Spirit lead me on level ground.

—PSALM 143:10

∽

Lord, where You lead, I will follow. I pray that You will take me from the slippery slope of my way and direct me toward the level landscape of Your will. Each day I want to seek Your teaching.

Let the lessons You have for me be apparent in the moment You are presenting them. Where I can learn from my past, please help me reflect on those times and heal so I can be whole, healthy, and ready to receive whatever is next.

What It Takes

Then he said to the crowd, "If any of you wants to be my follower, you must put aside your selfish ambition, shoulder your cross daily, and follow me. If you try to keep your life for yourself, you will lose it. But if you give up your life for me, you will find true life."

—LUKE 9:23-24 NLT

∽

Lord, You require me to leave behind my selfish ways and carry my cross in order to follow You. In contemporary times, this is a difficult concept. In my life, following can involve little commitment. I follow certain trends and then lose interest. I follow a leading sports team until the season is over. I follow teachings of my youth until they conflict with my adult pursuits.

But being one of Your children is a decision which involves my today, my tomorrow, and my eternity. Your mercy calls me and inspires me to give up my life. This is not a temporary interest; this is a passionate pursuit.

Model Behavior

Therefore, as God's chosen people, holy and dearly loved, clothe yourselves with compassion, kindness, humility, gentleness and patience. Bear with each other and forgive whatever grievances you may have against one another. Forgive as the Lord forgave you.

—COLOSSIANS 3:12-13

∞

God, when You place me in the presence of other people, I have a chance to lead by example...Your example. Give me a heart of compassion and kindness so I can reach out to other people with Your love. Grace me with patience and gentleness so I can reflect Your tenderness. And humble me before men so You are exalted.

When my own pride or agenda gets in the way of expressing You and Your feelings toward mankind, please correct me. Convict my spirit so I can repent. And with You as my witness, may I lead with a spirit of forgiveness to model Your greatest gift.

Marriage

Keeping the Faith

Another thing you do: You flood the LORD's altar with tears. You weep and wail because he no longer pays attention to your offerings or accepts them with pleasure from your hands. You ask, "Why?" It is because the LORD is acting as the witness between you and the wife of your youth, because you have broken faith with her, though she is your partner, the wife of your marriage covenant.

—MALACHI 2:13-14

∽

Lord, You hold my marriage up to see if it is holy and pleasing. You consider my actions toward my wife and consider this partnership to be sacred. When I am not caring for my wife as I should, You do not wish to hear my pleas for attention or fulfillment. If I shame my household, I have shamed You.

Create in me a giving, nurturing spirit toward my wife. May I respect her, adore her, and cherish her. Guard my heart so I never put this relationship at risk. As You watch me, Lord, may my words and deeds reflect faithfulness so I honor You and the wife of my youth forever.

Helpmates

Husbands, love your wives, just as Christ loved the church and gave himself up for her to make her holy, cleansing her by the washing with water through the word, and to present her to himself as a radiant church, without stain or wrinkle or any other blemish, but holy and blameless.

—EPHESIANS 5:25-27

∽

God, You created Eve to be Adam's helpmate. You saw that Adam would not be whole, would not be fulfilled without the one designed to complete him. Thank You, Lord, for establishing this relationship. I pray that I stay devoted to my wife, my companion, and love her without reservation.

I pray to be a caring, attentive man. Lord, keep me from ever causing my wife to sin. May my behavior keep her pure and radiant. May my words encourage and strengthen her faith in You. Lead me in Your ways so my commitment is righteous and never self-serving. Thank You for the love of my life.

Me, My Wife, and Thee

Two are better than one, because they have a good return for their work: If one falls down, his friend can help him up. But pity the man who falls and has no one to help him up!...A cord of three strands is not quickly broken.

—ECCLESIASTES 4:9-10,12

∽

Dear Lord, let me take the vows and ties of marriage seriously. This is such a big decision in my life. May I see, with Your eyes, the importance of such a covenant. I have spent many days on my own, enjoying solitude and the freedom of making decisions that primarily affect me. But I have also spent time thinking about how much stronger I would feel once I enter into a forever relationship.

When husbands and wives stay tethered to the cord of Your heartstrings, it becomes a strong lifeline. I want my spirit to be united in marriage, in faith, and in Your will, Lord.

Connection

Bad Connections

Do not let anyone who delights in false humility and the worship of angels disqualify you for the prize. Such a person goes into great detail about what he has seen, and his unspiritual mind puffs him up with idle notions. He has lost connection with the Head, from whom the whole body, supported and held together by its ligaments and sinews, grows as God causes it to grow.

—COLOSSIANS 2:18-19

༄

So often my mind will separate from the actions of my body, enlarging the gap between my will and Your will, Father. My head knows of Your will, but my body seems to disconnect and follow its own will. This loss of connection between my understanding and my action hurtles me through the gauntlet of frustration. The distance between me and You grows.

Eternal God, I pray for the restoration of my connection with You. Give me the spiritual wisdom to reclaim that glorious peace found in abiding in Your will.

Resurrection
of Relationship

*So, my brothers, you also died to the law through
the body of Christ, that you might belong to another,
to him who was raised from the dead, in order that
we might bear fruit to God.*

—ROMANS 7:4

The law calls to my attention rules, rules, and more
rules simply to be obeyed. I become so obsessed with
keeping and not breaking them that I have turned
myself inward. I have become self-centered and have
lost sight of my relationship with my Lord. The pain in
my heart makes me long for the times when I had more
hope.

O Lord, Your unselfishness gave us the power of the
resurrection in Jesus. I pray for a reconnection with my
Savior. Fill me again with the new life of the Spirit and
lead me away from my selfish ways.

Connections

From one man he made every nation of men, that they should inhabit the whole earth; and he determined the times set for them and the exact places where they should live. God did this so that men would seek him and perhaps reach out for him and find him, though he is not far from each one of us. "For in him we live and move and have our being." As some of your own poets have said, "We are his offspring."

—ACTS 17:26-28

♥

When I take my daily drive to work, I forget to notice Your presence in all of Your creations. How can those other drivers (especially the ones that ride my bumper or run the yellow lights) be children of Your creation? Why do I find myself so out of touch with Your other children? I forget that each one is created in Your image, and I become upset by their actions. I don't stop and think long enough to have a heart for them.

Lord of all creation and all people, I open myself to the workings of Your Spirit. Connect me to all of Your children. I dedicate myself to seeing Your touch in the world about me. With Your strength I will try to connect with everyone I meet this day.

Fellowship
and Faith

*We proclaim to you what we have seen and heard,
so that you also may have fellowship with us. And
our fellowship is with the Father and with his Son,
Jesus Christ. We write this to make our joy complete.*

—1 JOHN 1:3-4

∽

Scripture calls me to the joy of fellowship with other people, Jesus. It is so easy to become busy with trivial things and disconnect from people. If only I could realize that life without fellowship is unlivable, lonely, and not as You intended it to be for me. A solitary existence would limit my exposure to Your character and compassion as You express it through other individuals in the body of Christ.

God, I feel the need to connect with other people and with You. I pray for the strength to do so. I ask Your help in prioritizing my activities today so that I may experience fellowship with other believers. May my joy be complete.

Worry

Pass on the Cheer

An anxious heart weighs a man down, but a kind word cheers him up.

—PROVERBS 12:25

My God and Savior, I tremble with fear of what other people may think. And when someone expresses criticism or judgment toward me, I manage to wear my mask of indifference that hides the turmoil boiling inside. If only people knew the damage they do with their thoughtless words. I come to You with my pain, but I am unable to share my feelings with anyone else.

Lord, I know there are so many times when I speak without thinking and see the anguish in another person's eyes. Please, God, help me to find the good and kind word that will bring cheer to another. Then may I know peace through the joy of other people.

Giving Doubt a Rest

What does a man get for all the toil and anxious striving with which he labors under the sun? All his days his work is pain and grief; even at night his mind does not rest....A man can do nothing better than to eat and drink and find satisfaction in his work. This too, I see, is from the hand of God....To the man who pleases him, God gives wisdom, knowledge and happiness.

—ECCLESIASTES 2:22-26

∽

Oh, God, how many times do I toss and turn throughout the night wondering what I am doing? Why continue this constant cycle of effort and work? What am I missing? Surely there must be more than this! Where is the payoff? What about my reward?

Fill me with your Holy Spirit; ease my restless mind. Free me from these chains of worry and doubt! Father, please help me to enjoy each moment from day to day. Hold me steady to the task at hand so that I discover the satisfaction of a job well done. I thirst for Your wisdom and yearn for the day my mind rests in Your faithfulness.

In God I Trust

Therefore I tell you, do not worry about your life, what you will eat or what you will drink, or about your body, what you will wear....And can any of you by worrying add a single hour to your span of life?...Your heavenly Father knows that you need all these things. But strive first for the kingdom of God and his righteousness, and all these things will be given to you as well.

—MATTHEW 6:25,27,32-33 (NRSV)

∽

Lord, it's so hard *not* to focus on money. Sitting here at the kitchen table, I end up making myself sick with worry over these bills. It's never enough, Lord. What if something bad happens? What if I lose my job? What if the market crashes and we lose our retirement money? Our savings account would only last so long. Then what, Lord?

Dear gracious God, forgive me for not trusting You. Please strengthen my faith and help me to remember that no matter what situation life finds me in, You will be there with me. Despite my misgivings I need not worry, for Your will shall be done.

Fearless

Yet if you devote your heart to him and stretch out your hands to him, if you put away the sin that is in your hand and allow no evil to dwell in your tent, then you will lift up your face without shame; you will stand firm and without fear. You will surely forget your trouble, recalling it only as waters gone by. Life will be brighter than noonday, and darkness will become like morning. You will be secure, because there is hope; you will look about you and take your rest in safety.

—JOB 11:13-18

∞

God, I admit it: I get so caught up in the seeming importance of day-to-day adversities that I forget to call upon You. Opportunities to care for other people and seek Your guidance slip by me. Then something happens, and it is crisis time again. That is when I turn to You and plead for Your intervention. I promise to put Your will first, but this good intention doesn't last.

Oh, Lord, fill me with Your Spirit today. Let Him shake me to the core so that I think first of how You can be served, letting all else fall into place. Guide me in my day-to-day labors so my actions are led by You and my heart is filled with Your love. Soothe my soul so I feel secure walking along Your path.

Power

How to Be First

Jesus called them together and said, "You know that those who are regarded as rulers of the Gentiles lord it over them, and their high officials exercise authority over them. Not so with you. Instead, whoever wants to become great among you must be your servant, and whoever wants to be first must be slave of all. For even the Son of Man did not come to be served, but to serve, and to give his life as a ransom for many."

—MARK 10:42-45

ॐ

Dear Lord, thank You for helping me get to where I am today. I know that my life has been blessed with a number of successes. I admit that I like to do things my way. I don't like giving up control to someone else. I get so upset with people when they don't do as I say. I'm used to giving the orders, and I'm good at it. Please, God, help temper my small authority with humility and grace.

Almighty One, I am amazed at what Your Son was able to do for me. It is not easy to choose to be last. That competitive edge and drive to be first have been ingrained in me since my early years. Help me to find a way to put other people ahead of myself, to uplift my brothers and sisters, to be a true servant. Oh, Lord, help me resist having to be first.

Remind Me

But we have this treasure in jars of clay to show that this all-surpassing power is from God and not from us. We are hard pressed on every side, but not crushed; perplexed, but not in despair; persecuted, but not abandoned; struck down, but not destroyed. We always carry around in our body the death of Jesus, so that the life of Jesus may also be revealed in our body.

—2 CORINTHIANS 4:7-10

∽

Heavenly Father, remind me how much I live by Your power and not mine (although I admit that I don't really like the reminders—sometimes they overwhelm me). I know that when everything is going well, my pride can overtake me, and out comes my self-will.

Lord God, help me to remember that I don't have to do this all alone. Remind me to lean on Your power, to reach out for Jesus whenever I feel that I can no longer go the distance. Almighty God, help me to remember that Your power can lift me above any setback, and I have no need to fear.

Grace Is Enough

*Therefore, to keep me from being too elated, a thorn
was given me in the flesh....Three times I appealed
to the Lord about this, that it would leave me, but
he said to me, "My grace is sufficient for you, for
power is made perfect in weakness...." Therefore I
am content.*

—2 CORINTHIANS 12:7-12 (NRSV)

✍

God, if anyone should have been able to pray away
physical pain, it would have been the saintly Paul. Alas,
the thorn remained. Sometimes healings take place, but
often pain remains. When I or a loved one suffers, I
wonder, "Should I have prayed harder?" You call me to
come to You with my requests, yet it is not my place to
dictate Your will in any situation.

Lord, empower me even though I contract thorns in
my flesh and am doubled over with pain. Help me to
find contentment when I experience Your grand power.
Enable me to carry on in spite of illness and hardship.
May I know Your grace is sufficient for me. Thanks be
to God!

Power Over Sin

Therefore rid yourselves of all sordidness and rank growth of wickedness, and welcome with meekness the implanted word that has the power to save your souls. But be doers of the word, and not merely hearers who deceive themselves.

—JAMES 1:21-22 (NRSV)

∽

Dear God, how easy it is to get sucked into the depravity of humanity. Temptations pull ever so gently; the pressure remains at every turn. Sin emerges on the television, in books, magazines, and movies. I am bombarded by ideas that counter the values You ask me to hold dear.

Lord, I welcome Your Word. Fill me with the power to not only withstand, but also to move forward in service as well. Let me be one who dares to be different. Give me the strength to show other people Your Word through my actions. May they come to know You when they see You in me. This is my prayer.

Covenant

Promises, Promises

*And God said, "This is the sign of the covenant I am
making between me and you and every living crea-
ture with you, a covenant for all generations to
come: I have set my rainbow in the clouds, and it
will be the sign of the covenant between me and the
earth."*

—GENESIS 9:12-13

⁊

Lord, at times the rush of events obscures my
awareness that this world is Your world, even with the
traffic jams, lost keys, tax forms, sick children, and
backed-up sinks. If only I could remember to stop and
regroup every time I saw one of Your rainbows.

Maker of heaven and earth, may I receive the grace
to keep both life and living in perspective. Beyond the
storms, I thank You for the quiet arch in full color that
expands over all You have created and stands as a
reminder of Your promise to us.

As for Me and My House

But if serving the LORD seems undesirable to you, then choose for yourselves this day whom you will serve, whether the gods your forefathers served beyond the River, or the gods of the Amorites, in whose land you are living. But as for me and my household, we will serve the LORD.

—JOSHUA 24:15

∽

Almighty God, there are times when I slip and slide. You know how many times I have failed You. Often I stumble when I try to serve more than one master. I choose to serve objects of desire rather than following Your will, Your calling for me, or Your precepts.

I yearn for the day when my faith will stand strong and my service rest secure. Hold me steady and keep my path straight and true as I choose again to serve only You. Let me pass along this conviction to my household. Let me lead by example and please You.

Write Your Will on My Heart

*This is the [new] covenant I will make with the
house of Israel....I will put my law in their minds
and write it on their hearts. I will be their God, and
they will be my people.*

—JEREMIAH 31:33

&

Lord, if only I could have Your will and way so
written on my heart, in my inmost being, that I would
not have to ask, "Shall I do this, or shall I do that?" I
would know how to act without counting the cash or
seeking self-gain. How often do You long to write Your
will upon my life, yet come across my resistance, my
own strong will countering Your intention for good?
You call me to be Your own. Lord, help me run to Your
side and be named Your child, one of Your people.

I open my heart now to Your divine penmanship.
Lord, please write.

Receiving Your Promises

So do not throw away your confidence; it will be richly rewarded. You need to persevere so that when you have done the will of God, you will receive what he has promised.

—HEBREWS 10:35-36

∽

You have given me so much, Lord. My offering of thanks and a willing spirit seems so small compared to the expanse of Your mercy. Yet I have confidence that You receive the gift of my days with graciousness…it is Your way. I carry Your love with me through good and bad times; I pay attention to my blessings because they direct me back to the hand of the Giver.

Each day reveals the rewards of a faith lived out. I hunger for a deeper understanding of my purpose under heaven. Give me the courage to do Your will. Open up my heart and my life, Lord, so I can fully receive the promises You have for me.